REPORTS

OF

J. N. Campbell, J. C. Wright, and L. S. Chatfield;

AND OF

David Buel, Jr. and P. S. Van Rensselaer,

OF THE COMMISSION TO EXAMINE INTO THE PECUNIARY AFFAIRS OF

UNION COLLEGE.

ALSO,

THE MEMORIALS

OF THE PRESIDENT AND TRUSTEES OF THE COLLEGE IN REFERENCE TO SAID REPORTS.

SCHENECTADY:
RIGGS, PRINTER—STATE-STREET.

1853.

REPORT

OF THE MAJORITY OF THE COMMISSIONERS TO EXAMINE THE AFFAIRS OF UNION COLLEGE.

MADE TO THE SENATE, MARCH 4, 1853.

At a meeting of the commission on the affairs of Union College, held this day, March 1, 1853, were present the Comptroller, Judge Buel, P. S. Van Rensselaer and J. N. Campbell, when it was agreed by the undersigned (Judge Buel and Mr. Van Rensselaer dissenting,) to send into the Senate the following report, viz:

To the Senate of the State of New-York:

The undersigned, members of the commission appointed by the resolution of the Senate adopted April 12th, 1851, "to examine into the pecuniary affairs of Union College, and report upon the same," respectfully submit the statement, under oath, of their accountant herewith transmitted. This statement is the result of the examination made by the accountant of the books and vouchers of Union College, delivered to him by the officers of the College, and is believed by the undersigned to be a true and full exhibit of the pecuniary condition of that institution as presented by said books and vouchers, as authenticated annually by the treasurer thereof.

From this statement it appears that the whole amount received by the College is,

Original grants and endowments,	$ 41,258 73½
Grants and endowments by the Legislature,	704,836 64
Bequests and donations,	785 00
Sale of old college buildings,	78,766 79½
Revenue above expenses,	432,095 61
	$1,257,742 78

Whole amount of property now held by the College.

College buildings, real estate, library and apparatus,	$197,279 94½
Investments,	142,321 18½

Liabilities.

Permanent fund, ...	$138,656 44
Grants for library and apparatus unexpended, ...	17,648 04
For revenue, ...	57,906 51½
Debt, ...	21,260 07
	$235,471 06½
To meet which investments, ...	142,321 18½
Deficiency, ...	$93,149 88

President's indebtedness.

Hunter and Stuyvesant property, ...	$184,256 06
Interest, ...	184,770 13
Other debts, ...	191,509 40
Interest, ...	322,254 05
	$885,789 62

President's receipts from Yates & McIntyre from lotteries, independently of college lotteries, ...	$192,199 94
From Union College, exclusive of President's fund, . .	107,687 44
	$299,887 38

J. N. CAMPBELL.
JOHN C. WRIGHT.

I have cursorily examined the balance sheets and statements of the accountant employed by the commissioners appointed to examine into the pecuniary affairs of Union College, and concur in the above report.

L. S. CHATFIELD.

REPORT

OF THE MINORITY OF THE COMMISSIONERS APPOINTED TO EXAMINE THE AFFAIRS OF UNION COLLEGE.

To the Honorable the Senate of the State of New-York:

The undersigned, two of the commissioners appointed to enquire into the pecuniary affairs of Union College, by a resolution of the Senate of the 3d July, 1851, to join a commission previously appointed by a resolution of the 12th April, 1851, and specially instructed in respect to their duties, by a resolution of the 28th June, 1851, respectfully ask leave to express their dissent from the action of two of their number, not constituting a majority, in presenting to the Senate the statements of the accountant employed by them to examine the books of Union College.

By the terms of the said resolutions, the undersigned can not but understand that the commissioners were not only to employ an accountant to examine the books and accounts of the College, and prepare statements exhibiting the results of such examinations, but they were bound to verify those statements and results themselves, and to investigate and report in the terms of the resolution of 28th June, "whether the funds granted by the State have been duly applied to the objects specified in the respective grants," "whether the permanent funds so granted remain entire and are safely invested," "whether any funds belonging to the College have been applied to any personal purpose by the President, or any other officer or person," "whether any and what losses have occurred in the management of the College, and the cause of such losses," and "whether the President or any other officer has participated in the profits of any lotteries which were appropriated by the acts granting such lotteries to Union College."

The requirement to report on all these points, implies by the very force of the term, that the commission were to form and express their own convictions from an examination of the evidence.

The undersigned can not suppose that two of the highest executive officers of the State and three Regents of the University, were commissioned merely to appoint an accountant and transmit the result of his labors to the Senate—a duty that might as well be performed by the president or secretary of the Senate.

On the first of March, inst., the first meeting of the commissioners, since the completion of the accountant's duties, was held, at which four of them were present, and at which the statement and schedules, which the accountant thought it necessary to make, were laid before them.—These statements and schedules are quite voluminous, and the undersigned have had no sufficient opportunity to examine them and form any opinion of the principles upon which they have been made out, or the data on which they are founded; nor was there any explanation of those principles and data given to the commission.

The resolutions require the commission, or a majority of them, to visit the college and examine its officers and other persons, touching the subjects to be investigated. This duty has not been performed by any of the commission, although invited by a letter of July 23d, 1851, from a committee of the trustees to do so, and to apprise the committee of the time and place of such meeting, and proffering their assistance in the investigation.

Neither the president nor the trustees have had any opportunity of examining the statements and schedules submitted by the accountant, or of making any explanation of them, or showing any errors therein; and previous to the last meeting of the commission on the 1st of March, inst., another letter was received from the committee of the trustees, soliciting an opportunity for such examination.

The undersigned were desirous of affording them such an opportunity, but the two members of the commission above referred to, refused to afford such an opportunity, and insisted upon transmitting to your honorable body, the statements and schedules as prepared by the accountant.

To this course the undersigned could not assent for the reasons above given, and they wish by this communication to exonerate themselves from the responsibility of such a proceeding.

DAVID BUEL, Jr.
P. S. VAN RENSSELAER.

Albany, March 3d, 1853.

MEMORIAL

OF THE PRESIDENT OF UNION COLLEGE.

To the Honorable the Senate of the State of New-York:

The memorial of the undersigned, president of Union College, respectfully showeth,

That on the 12th of March, 1849, the members of the committee on colleges, of which the Hon. James W. Beekman was a member, procured the passage of resolutions in the Assembly, requiring a fiscal report from the trustees of Union College.

That report was made, and the same committee, of which Mr. Beekman was a member, were directed to visit the college, and report the result of their examination to the subsequent Legislature. That duty was performed, and the committee disagreeing, two reports were made, the one by Mr. Beekman, censuring the president and trustees; the other by Mr. Pruyn, defending the conduct of both.

To the charges in the report of Mr. Beekman, the treasurer of Union College replied, and in so satisfactory a manner, that the Assembly refused to take any further notice of the charges contained therein.

On being informed of this, Mr. Beekman, who in the meantime had become a member of the Senate, moved in that body a resolution requiring the Comptroller and Attorney General to examine and report on the fiscal condition of said college.

On the 7th of February, 1851, the Comptroller reported to the Senate, that he had been unable to attend to the duty assigned him.

On motion of the Hon. Senator Beekman, this report of the Comptroller was referred to the committee on literature, of which the Hon. Senator Beekman was chairman.

On the 12th of April, the Hon. Senator Beekman, without giving any intimation of his purpose, made an elaborate report, in which the charges previously made by him in the Assembly were repeated, new charges added, and the conclusion previously arrived at, re-asserted, to wit: "*That the fiscal condition of Union College is unsound and improper;*" and having made this report, he moved "that the Comptroller, the Attorney-General, and John N. Campbell, one of the Regents of the University, have power to employ a skilful accountant, and send for persons and papers, to examine into the pecuniary affairs of Union College, and report upon the same to the next Legislature." (Senate Journal, 1851, page 526.)

This ex parte report made by Senator Beekman at the very close of the session, was printed, and many extra copies of it gratuitously circulated throughout the country.

To the charges made and delinquencies set forth therein, as soon as a copy thereof could be obtained, an answer was prepared and ordered to be published.

At the extra session of the Legislature convened in June following, a resolution was, at the instance of the trustees, passed by the Senate, directing the commissioners themselves, personally to visit the college, *re-examine* the proceedings already had, and to investigate and report to the Legislature on five specific points, derived from the general and sweeping violations of trust imputed in the report in question, to wit:

"1. Whether the funds granted by the State to Union College have been duly applied to the objects specified in the respective grants:

"2. Whether the permanent funds so granted remain entire, and are safely invested:

"3. Whether any funds belonging to the college have been applied to any personal purpose by the president, or any other officer or person:

"4. Whether any and what losses have occurred in the management of the college funds, and the causes of such losses:

"5. Whether the president, or any other officer, has, while in the employment of the college, participated individually in the profits of any lotteries which were appropriated, by the acts granting such lotteries, to Union College; and that the commission appointed by the resolution referred to, or a majority of them, be empowered to employ some person authorised by law to administer an oath to persons examined by such commission."

And two additional members, Messrs. Buel and Van Rensselaer, were added to the commission.

As there now seemed to be a reasonable prospect that in place of another private ex parte inquest and condemnation, on vague and sweeping imputations, a fair and open trial on specific and previously stated charges, was at length to be obtained, the undersigned at once suspended the printing of the answer to Senator Beekman's ex parte report, and placed the books of the college at the disposal of the accountant appointed by the commission.

Both these acts were performed by the undersigned, on his own responsibility, and contrary to the expressed opinion of the legal members of the board, who insisted that an examination of the same, by an accountant entirely ignorant of the transactions concerned, exposed to the influence of the accusing party, and in the absence of the party accused, could not be expected to be either correct or impartial.

Not partaking in these forebodings, and knowing that the books contained nothing that any trustee or officer of the college wished to have concealed, the undersigned, desirous of a thorough examination of the same, and an impartial exhibition before the public, of the contents thereof, called on the chairman, and afterwards on other members of the commission, and stated what he had done ; and added that when the accountant was through with examining the college books, the undersigned would place confidentially his own books, which contained still fuller accounts of the transactions complained of, at the disposal of the commissioners for examination, that nothing would be concealed, but on the contrary every facility furnished for becoming acquainted with the entire truth ; and that in place of publishing the answer, already in the press, to the charges which had been preferred, the same would, after having subjoined thereto the requisite supplementary evidence, be presented to the commissioners as a part of the answer of the trustees.

And finally, that what the trustees desired was, that a thorough examination might be had, and that they might have an opportunity to meet their accusers face to face, to reply to the charges made, and explain the difficulties that might require explanation.

The chairman approved of the course adopted and assured the undersigned as he did another trustee, that a thorough examination should be made by himself, and that when the accountant was through with the books, the commissioners would visit the college, make the requisite personal enquiries, and give the trustees the requisite opportunity for meeting the charges made against them and explaining the difficulties which might arise, and added to the undersigned that the answer prepared to said charges, if presented to them as proposed, should be presented with their report to the Senate. Similar communications were made to other members of the commission and similar assurances received by the undersigned and by other members of the board of trustees.

The same communications made to the chairman and other members of the commission, were also made to the accountant; and an assurance was given by him that if any difficulties were met with, they should be presented to the trustees for explanation, and that the result of his examination should be exhibited to the trustees for examination before the same was presented to the commissioners for action.

And just before the accountant finished his labors, the undersigned received from him information of the fact, accompanied by the assurance that he was now coming to Schenectady, and should bring with him the schedules which contained the result of his labors for examination and comparison. Nor was a doubt entertained that this would be the case, till informed by the public papers that his statements had been made and acted on by the commissioners, transmitted to the Senate, and ordered to be printed. The course adopted in this examination will neither be made the subject of comment or complaint, though not precisely such as the undersigned, under a change of circumstances, would have felt himself at liberty to pursue.

Still it may be permitted him to add that if any such balance as is stated in the report of the commission exists against him, or indeed, if any balance whatever, the trustees, the president and the treasurer will, it is hoped, be pardoned for not having themselves discovered it, since no traces of its existence will be found to exist in any books of the college delivered to the accountant for examination, or in any other books ever in their possession, or known by them to exist elsewhere; and though guided by all the lights which a personal transaction of the business afforded, they have hitherto supposed that the college was indebted to its president, and not its president to the college; still, were it otherwise, and were evidence furnished that any indebtedness on his part existed, either in law or equity, no matter whence that evidence was derived, he should meet it cheerfully. And this the more cheerfully, as the amount, whatever the same might be, would go to augment the resources of an institution in the furtherance of whose interests he has spent the greater portion of his life.

That there are outside the college books, unliquidated items of account connected with other accounts not yet in a state for liquidation, kept partly by the treasurer as directed by the board, and more fully by the president, in relation to property gratuitously set apart by him, and by him secured to the ultimate use of Union College or some kindred institution connected therewith, are facts which though not hitherto desired by him to be made public, can not be denied. The right of supervizing and controlling this property during the natural life of the president, has been reserved by him. Still the aid of the treasurer and of the finance committee in this behalf has often been required, and the trustees generally have been kept confidentially informed in relation thereto. All which matters, though as yet private and confidential, have together with the books and documents in relation thereto, been submitted for the satisfaction of the successive committees heretofore appointed to examine into the fiscal affairs of Union College ; and all which matters and the books and documents in relation thereto would in like manner have been submitted to this commission, had an opportunity for doing this been afforded, as the undersigned, as well as other members of the board, were assured would be the case.

Were even these unliquidated accounts examined, and the debits and credits as they exist therein, truly transferred to the balance sheet made out from the books, or were the balance sheet of the books as the bebits and credits exist there, truly exhibited by itself, it would change the whole aspect of the expose now made public, and present the undersigned, as is well known to those conversant with the fiscal concerns of the college to be the case, not as a debtor but a creditor of the same.

But with respect to debits which have never been known to have existence in any previously existing books of account, introduced arbitrarily and in the absence of both the parties concerned, and without the knowledge of either, into a final balance sheet, if any reply were necessary, it could only be made by a simple and explicit denial of their having any foundation in truth.

Since these things are so, it is not perceived on what principle of public justice or private expediency it has been deemed proper to make a false issue, and disturb the public mind by an apprehension of the misapplication of trust funds, which apprehension the ultimate publication of the truth and the whole truth, must dissipate for ever.

It is painful to the undersigned to speak thus, or to speak at all on a subject on which he had hoped to have been permitted to remain silent, till the revelations of the tomb should have silenced calumny and rendered inquiry for ever thereafter unnecessary.

But since this has not been permitted, and since nothing but the truth which has been perhaps too long withheld, will disabuse the public mind of the slanders which have been so long and so industriously circulated, and since neither the trustees nor the undersigned have been permitted, as promised, to present their answer to the charges heretofore made, it is confidently expected that the Senate will, as an act of justice to both, appoint an impartial committee from their own body, before whom the undersigned may appear, with the trustees of the college, and answer to the charges heretofore made, as well as to the charges now made in the ex parte report of a portion of the late commission. All which is respectfully submitted,

ELIPHALET NOTT.

March 16, 1853.

MEMORIAL

OF THE TRUSTEES OF UNION COLLEGE.

To the Hon. the Senate of the State of New-York:

The memorial of the undersigned, the treasurer of Union College, in behalf of the trustees, respectfully shows,

That they have learned by the public newspapers that voluminous statements and schedules have been laid before your honorable body, purporting to be the results of an examination into the pecuniary affairs of Union College by Mr. Vanderheyden, an accountant appointed by a commission constituted by your honorable body in 1851.

That the said commission was organized upon, and in consequence of a report of the literature committee, of which the Hon. Mr. Beekman was chairman ; that the said report was made upon an ex parte examination, without any opportunity to any trustee or officer of the college to explain or correct any of the statements therein contained, and at so late a period of the session of the Senate, that there was no time for any examination thereof and reply thereto.

That the said commission, in June and July, 1851, was augmented, and special instructions to enquire into and report upon certain specific points were given, and they or a majority of them were required personally to visit the college and re-examine the proceedings theretofore had in relation thereto, and investigate the facts, and were authorized to employ a proper officer to administer oaths to the persons examined by them. And that thereupon, in July, 1851, a committee of the trustees of Union College, specially appointed for that purpose, addressed a letter to each of the commissioners, professing their readiness to enter on the investigation, their desire that it should be prompt, and soliciting the appointment of a time and place for the meeting of the commissioners.* That no answer was given to the said application, except by two of the commission, Messrs. Buel and Van Rensselaer; that no time for a meeting of the commission had been appointed, and their readiness to attend one when called.

* See note, page 16

That an accountant was appointed to examine the books of account of the college; that he and an assistant have been engaged in such examination, in searching for evidence in other quarters, and in copying from the public records of Schenectady county. That neither the accountant or his assistant has sought for any explanation from the treasurer or any other officer or trustee of the college, in reference to the matters of enquiry committed to them. Mr. Vanderheyden some months since, and repeatedly afterwards, voluntarily informed the acting treasurer and the acting register of the college that he would call upon the president, when he arrived at the subject of the lotteries, for information and explanations; and he has made similar communications by letter and otherwise, and that he would visit the college and submit to the president, for examination, his schedules, before the same were submitted to the commissioners for their action thereon. That this information was communicated to the trustees, who refrained from any movement on the subject, in full faith that they would have ample opportunity to examine the said statements before they were submitted for the action of the commission.

That such statements were never submitted to the treasurer or any officer of the college, and the trustees have had no opportunity of examining them.

That some of the trustees having learned that the said statements had been submitted to the commission, and that a meeting of that board was to be held to consider them, in the early part of the present month of March, previous to such meeting addressed a letter to each of the commissioners, soliciting an opportunity of being heard by the board in explanation of the said statements, and to correct them, if necessary, before they should be acted upon by them, and sent to the Senate.

No such opportunity has been afforded to the undersigned, or any officer or trustee of the college; nor have any of the commissioners, to the knowledge of the undersigned, visited the college or examined any of its officers. Yet the said statements, as the undersigned learns from the public newspapers, have been transmitted to the Senate by a majority of the commission, in opposition to the opinions of two of their number, and have been ordered to be printed.

The trustees earnestly desire a full and thorough examination of their pecuniary affairs, believing as they confidently do, that it will result in the entire refutation of the calumnies that have been circulated on that subject; and they claim an opportunity to explain and correct the said statements before a disinterested and impartial committee of your honorable body, which cannot well now decline proceeding with and completing the investigation into the several specific subjects ordered to be enquired into and reported on, by yourselves.

They therefore pray the appointment of such a committee, who will possess legal authority to compel the attendance of witnesses, and the production of papers, which has become the more necessary from the secret and ex parte examinations which the undersigned learns have been made by Mr. Vanderheyden, under the authority of the chairman of the commission.

ALEX. HOLLAND,
Treasurer of Union College.

March 12, 1853.

NOTE.

UNION COLLEGE,
Schenectady, July 23, 1851.

GENTLEMEN,—The undersigned have been appointed by the trustees of Union College to attend before you and assist in the investigation of charges which have been made and extensively circulated, and which are calculated to impair the confidence of the public in the institution, and to injuriously affect the reputation of its venerable and distinguished President. Believing, as the Board of Trustees do, that these charges have no foundation in truth, they are anxious that a speedy as well as full examination of the subject should be had. We therefore request that the earliest practicable day should be appointed by you to commence the investigation, and that all the investigating commissioners should attend thereon. We also desire to be informed of the time and place of meeting, and that the members of the Senate committee by whom the charges have been brought before the public, should also have notice, and that they be requested to furnish with the evidence upon which the report was based, and the sources of information to which you are to apply for evidence in support of the charges contained in their report.

Permit us to suggest, that if the convenience of the commissioners should render it necessary to carry on the investigation at any place other than the College, that such investigation may take place during the present vacation, as it will be necessary that several officers of the College should be present to give the requisite explanations of complicated accounts which have run through more than half a century, and such officers cannot be spared from their duties from the College during the collegiate terms, to attend the meeting of the commissioners at any other place without serious detriment to the institution.

We are with respect, yours, &c.

R. H. WALWORTH,
R. M. BLATCHFORD,
A. HUNT,
B. R. WOOD.

Revd. Dr. JOHN N. CAMPBELL, PHILO C. FULLER, L. S. CHATFIELD, P. S. VAN RENSSELAER, DAVID BUEL, JUN. Esqrs.

Commissioners.

www.ingramcontent.com/pod-product-compliance
Lightning Source LLC
LaVergne TN
LVHW020643110826
845149LV00004B/1328